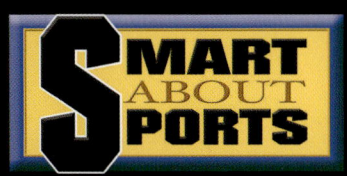

Soccer in Eastern Europe

By
Mike Kennedy
with Mark Stewart

NORWOOD HOUSE  PRESS

Norwood House Press, P.O. Box 316598, Chicago, Illinois 60631

For information regarding Norwood House Press,
please visit our website at: www.norwoodhousepress.com or call 866-565-2900.

Photo Credits:
   All interior photos provided by Getty Images, except Page 15) Black Book Partners archives.
Cover Photos:
   Top Left: Panini.
   Top Right: Michel Krakowski/AFP/Getty Images.
   Bottom Left: Christopher Lee/Getty Images.
   Bottom Right: Merlin/Futera FZ LLC.
The soccer memorabilia photographed for this book is part of the authors' collections:
   Page 10) Novakovic: Panini.
   Page 12) Puskas: Sporting Publications Ltd.; Yashin: Rekord; Masopust: The Sun/News Group Newspapers Ltd.;
      Boniek: Dandy Football Bubblegum.
   Page 13) Hagi: Brooke Bond & Co.; Stoichkov: Merlin/Topps Europe Ltd.; Suker: Trebor Barratt Ltd.;
      Shevchenko: Futera FZ LLC.

Designer: Ron Jaffe
Project Management: Black Book Partners, LLC
Editorial Production: Jessica McCulloch
Special thanks to Ben and Bill Gould

Library of Congress Cataloging-in-Publication Data
   Kennedy, Mike, 1965-
      Soccer in Eastern Europe / by Mike Kennedy, with Mark Stewart.
         p. cm. -- (Smart about sports)
      Includes bibliographical references and index.
      Summary: "An introductory look at soccer teams and their fans in countries
   in eastern Europe including Czech Republic, Poland, and Russia. Includes a
   brief history, facts, photos, records, and glossary"--Provided by publisher.
     ISBN-13: 978-1-59953-445-9 (library edition : alk. paper)
     ISBN-10: 1-59953-445-2 (library edition : alk. paper)
    1. Soccer--Europe, Eastern--Juvenile literature. 2. Soccer teams--Europe,
   Eastern--Juvenile literature. I. Stewart, Mark, 1960- II. Title.
   GV944.E852K46 2011
   796.3340947--dc22
                                             2010045977

© 2011 by Norwood House Press. All rights reserved.
No part of this book may be reproduced without written permission from the publisher.

Manufactured in the United States of America in North Mankato, Minnesota.
170N–012011

Contents

Where in the World? 5
Once Upon a Time 6
At the Stadium 9
Town & Country 10
Shoe Box 12
Can't Touch This 14
Just For Kicks 17
On the Map 18
Stop Action 20
We Won! 22
Soccer Words 24
Index 24
Learn More 24

Words in **bold type** are defined on page 24.

Players from Ukraine show their team spirit.

Where in the World?

The people of Eastern Europe love soccer. For a long time, teams and players in the East were not allowed to play against the West. This is no longer the case. That is why European soccer is better than ever!

Once Upon a Time

Soccer came to Eastern Europe more than 100 years ago. In the 1950s, Hungary's team had the best players in the world. Fans called them the "Magical Magyars."

The Magical Magyars pose for a team photo in the 1950s.

Balloons rise from the field of Luzhniki Stadium.

At the Stadium

One of the best places to watch soccer is Luzhniki Stadium in Russia. Luzhniki means "puddles" in Russian. The stadium was built on ground that used to be very wet.

Town & Country

The best players from Eastern Europe often wear two uniforms. For example, Milivoje Novakovic played for a **club** in Germany in 2010. When his home country of Slovenia played, he joined the **national team**.

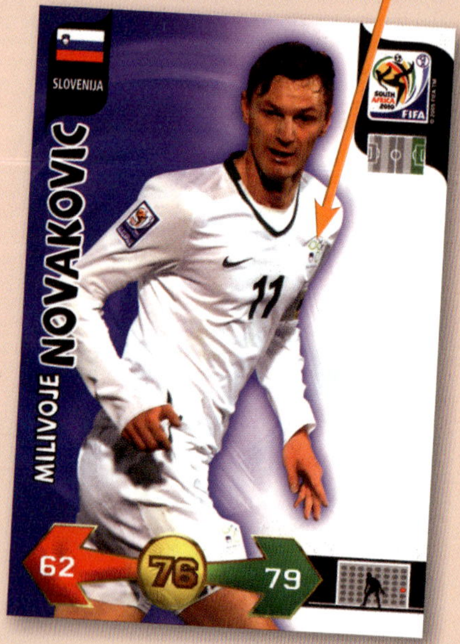

Milivoje Novakovic plays for his German team.

Shoe Box

The sports collection on these pages belongs to the authors. It shows some of the top Eastern European soccer stars.

Ferenc Puskas
Forward • Hungary
Ferenc Puskas scored more than 500 goals.

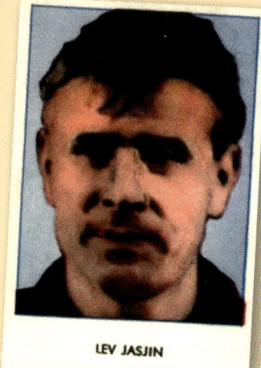

Lev Yashin
Goalkeeper • Russia
Many fans think Lev Yashin was the best goalkeeper ever.

Josef Masopust
Midfielder • Czech Republic
Josef Masopust was Europe's Player of the Year in 1962.

Zbigniew Boniek
Striker • Poland
"Zibi" Boniek was very fast and very hard to stop.

12

Gheorghe Hagi
Midfielder • Romania
Taking the ball away from Gheorghe Hagi was very hard to do.

Hristo Stoichkov
Forward • Bulgaria
Hristo Stoichkov was known as "The Dagger." He could cut right through the defense.

Davor Suker
Striker • Croatia
Davor Suker scored six goals during the 1998 **World Cup**.

Andriy Shevchenko
Striker • Ukraine
Andriy Shevchenko could always find open space near the goal.

Can't Touch This

Goalkeepers are the only players on the field allowed to use their hands. Touching the ball with just a fingertip can keep the ball out of the net. Sometimes the difference between a goal and a "save" is very small!

A Russian goalkeeper stretches to stop a shot.

Bulgaria sets up a wall to defend a free kick.

Just For Kicks

Watching soccer is more fun when you know some of the rules:

- On a **free kick**, the players on defense stand together to make a wall.

- The wall must be 30 feet (9.1 meters) from the kicker.

- A player can ask the referee to check the distance of the wall.

- The wall can be straight or curved.

On the Map

Girls and boys play soccer all over Eastern Europe, including these countries:

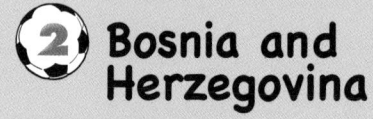

1. Belarus
2. Bosnia and Herzegovina
3. Bulgaria
4. Croatia
5. Czech Republic
6. Hungary
7. Montenegro
8. Poland
9. Romania
10. Russia
11. Serbia
12. Slovakia
13. Slovenia
14. Ukraine

Many countries have their own soccer stamps!

19

Stop Action

Lucie Heroldova of the Czech Republic makes a "tackle."

A tackle means sliding down to kick the ball away from another player.

20

Every player on a team wears a different number.

All players wear shin guards.

21

We Won!

Eastern Europe has some of the best teams in the world!

Men's Soccer	European Champion	Olympic* Champion
Hungary		1952, 1964, & 1968
Soviet Union	1960	1956 & 1988
Yugoslavia		1960
Poland		1972
East Germany		1976
Czechoslovakia	1976	1980

* The Olympics are a worldwide sports competition. Soccer has been part of the Olympics since 1900.

Members of the Soviet Union team wear their medals in 1988.

Change Comes to Eastern Europe

In the 1990s, the Soviet Union became 15 different countries, including Russia, Ukraine, and Belarus. Czechoslovakia became the Czech Republic and Slovakia. Yugoslavia became seven different countries, including Serbia, Croatia, and Slovenia. East Germany became a part of Germany.

23

Soccer Words

CLUB
Another word for team.

FREE KICK
A shot given to a team after a foul has been called.

NATIONAL TEAM
A team made up of players from the same country.

WORLD CUP
The tournament that decides the world champion of soccer. The World Cup is played every four years.

Index

Boniek, Zbigniew	12, **12**
Hagi, Gheorghe	13, **13**
Heroldova, Lucie	**20**
Masopust, Josef	12, **12**
Novakovic, Milivoje	10, **10**, **11**
Puskas, Ferenc	12, **12**
Shevchenko, Andriy	13, **13**
Stoichkov, Hristo	13, **13**
Suker, Davor	13, **13**
Yashin, Lev	12, **12**

Photos are on **bold** numbered pages.

Learn More

Learn more about the World Cup at www.fifa.com

Learn more about men's soccer at www.mlssoccer.com

Learn more about women's soccer at www.womensprosoccer.com